STUDY GUIDE

Farewell to Manzanar

Jeanne Wakatsuki Houston and
James D. Houston

WITH CONNECTIONS

HOLT, RINEHART AND WINSTON
Harcourt Brace & Company

Austin • New York • Orlando • Atlanta • San Francisco • Boston • Dallas • Toronto • London

Staff Credits

Associate Director: Mescal Evler

Manager of Editorial Operations: Robert R. Hoyt

Managing Editor: Bill Wahlgren

Executive Editor: Emily Shenk

Editorial Staff: *Assistant Managing Editor,* Mandy Beard; *Copyediting Supervisor,* Michael Neibergall; *Senior Copyeditor,* Mary Malone; *Copyeditors,* Joel Bourgeois, Jon Hall, Jeffrey T. Holt, Jane M. Kominek, Susan Sandoval; *Editorial Coordinators,* Marie H. Price, Jill Chertudi, Mark Holland, Marcus Johnson, Tracy DeMont; *Support Staff,* Pat Stover, Matthew Villalobos; *Word Processors,* Ruth Hooker, Margaret Sanchez, Kelly Keeley

Permissions: Carrie Jones, Catherine Paré

Design: *Art Director, Book & Media Design,* Joe Melomo

Image Services: *Art Buyer, Supervisor,* Elaine Tate

Prepress Production: Beth Prevelige, Sergio Durante

Manufacturing Coordinator: Michael Roche

Development Coordinator: Diane B. Engel

Cover Photograph: Camelot / Photonica

HRW is a registered trademark licensed to Holt, Rinehart and Winston.

Printed in the United States of America

ISBN 0-03-054354-1

123456 085 02 01 00 99 98

TABLE *of* CONTENTS

Using This Study Guide

This Study Guide is intended to

- *help students become active and engaged readers*
- *deepen students' enjoyment and understanding of literature*
- *provide you with multiple options for guiding students through the book and the Connections and for evaluating students' progress*

Most of the pages in this Study Guide are reproducible so that you can, if you choose, give students the opportunity to work independently.

Key Elements

- plot summary and analysis
- major themes
- character summaries
- notes on setting, point of view, and other literary elements

Making Meanings

- First Thoughts
- Shaping Interpretations
- Connecting with the Text
- Extending the Text
- Challenging the Text

A **Reading Check** focuses on review and comprehension.

The Worksheets

- **Reading Skills and Strategies Worksheets** focus on reading and critical-thinking strategies and skills.
- **Literary Elements Worksheets** guide students in considering and analyzing literary elements (discussed in **Key Elements**) important to understanding the book.
- **Vocabulary Worksheets** provide practice with Vocabulary Words. Activities target synonyms, affixes, roots, context clues, and other vocabulary elements.

For the Teacher

About the Writers Biographical highlights supplement the author biography that appears in the HRW Library edition of this book. Sidebars list works by and about the writer as resources for teaching and for students' research.

About the Book A critical history summarizes responses to the book, including excerpts from reviews. Sidebars suggest audiovisual and multimedia resources.

Key Elements Significant literary elements of the book are introduced. These elements recur in the questions, activities, worksheets, and assessment tools.

For the Student: reproducible masters

Before You Read: Activities *(preparation for beginning the book)* Motivating activities lead students to explore ideas and topics they will encounter in the book.

Making Meanings *(for each section of the book)* Questions move students from immediate personal response to high-level critical thinking.

Choices: Building Your Portfolio *(for each section of the book)* The activities suggested here involve students in exploring different aspects of the book on their own or collaboratively. The results may be included in a portfolio, developed further, or used as springboards for larger projects.

Book Projects *(culminating activities)* Cross-Curricular, Multimedia, and Internet projects relate to the book as a whole. Project ideas can be adapted for individual, pair, or group presentations.

Exploring the Connections *(a set of Making Meanings questions for each of the Connections readings)* Questions encourage students to relate the readings to the themes and topics of the book.

Story Notes *(multiple issues)* These one-page news sheets provide high-interest background information relating to historical, cultural, literary, and other elements of the book. They are intended for distribution *after* students have begun the book section the issue supplements.

Reading Skills and Strategies Worksheets *(one for each section of the book, plus a Book Organizer)*

Literary Elements Worksheets *(end of book)*

Vocabulary Worksheets *(during or after reading)*

Glossary, with Vocabulary Words *(to use throughout the book)* This list of words from the book serves as a mini-dictionary that students may refer to as they read. **Highlighted Vocabulary Words** support vocabulary acquisition.

Test *(end of book)* A mix of objective and short-answer questions covering the whole book provides a traditional form of assessment. Essay questions consist of five optional writing prompts.

Tips for Classroom Management

Preparing Students for Reading

Set aside a time each week for talking about books. On the right are some ideas for introducing a book and motivating students to pick it up and begin reading.

Reading and Responding

Book groups Although most students will read independently, discussions with classmates can enrich their reading enormously. This Study Guide suggests appropriate points to stop and talk about the story so far. At these stopping points, the **Making Meanings** questions can be used as discussion starters. Ask groups to keep a simple log of their discussions.

Full-class discussions Engage students by beginning the discussion with a question that encourages a personal response (see **First Thoughts** in **Making Meanings**). As students respond to the questions involving interpretation, invite them to support their inferences and conclusions with evidence from the text. Encourage a noncritical environment. Show your own enthusiasm for the book—it's infectious!

Reader's logs Logs, journals, and notebooks offer an open and nonthreatening yet systematic mode for students to respond in writing to the book. Making entries as they read can help students learn more about themselves as readers, monitor their own progress, and write more easily and fluently. Keeping logs can also enhance participation in small-group and class discussions of the book. Consider dialogue journals in which two readers—a student and you, a classmate, or a family member—exchange thoughts about their reading. **Reader's Log** suggestions appear in each issue of **Story Notes.**

Cooperative learning Small groups may meet both to discuss the book and to plan and work on projects related to the book (see ideas in **Choices** and in **Book Projects**). Encourage full participation by making sure that each group member has a defined role and that the roles rotate so that the same student is not always the leader or the recorder, for example.

Projects While students' projects can extend into other content areas, they should always contribute to enriching and extending students' understanding of the book itself. If students know when they begin the book that presenting a project will be a part of their evaluation, they can begin early to brainstorm, discuss, and try out ideas. Project ideas can come from **Story Notes,** from the **Choices** activities, from the **Book Projects** ideas, and, of course, from the students themselves. Projects can be developed and presented by individuals, pairs, or groups.

Reflecting

When students finish the book, they should not be left with a test as the culminating experience. Project presentations can be a kind of celebration, as can a concluding discussion. On the right are some ideas for a reflective discussion. They can be used in a whole-class environment, or small groups can choose certain questions to answer and share their conclusions (or their disagreements) with the class.

Ideas for Introducing the Book

- Give a brief book talk to arouse students' curiosity and interest (see **About the Book** for ideas).

- Play or show a segment of an audio, film, or video version of the book or an interview with the writer.

- Present high-interest biographical information about the writer (see **About the Writers** in this Study Guide and the biographical sketch at the end of the HRW Library edition of this book).

- Read aloud a passage from the book that arouses your own interest, and elicit predictions, inferences, and speculations from students.

- Lead a focused class discussion or suggest activities that (1) draw on students' prior knowledge or (2) lead them to generate their own ideas about a significant topic or theme they will encounter in the book (see **Before You Read).**

Reader's Log Starters

- When I began reading this book, I thought…
- My favorite part, so far, is…
- I predict that…
- I like the way the writer…
- I'd like to ask the writer…
- If I had written this book, I would have…
- This [character, incident, idea] reminds me of…
- This book made me think about…
- This book made me realize…

Questions for Reflection

- What was your favorite part of the book (and why)?

- If you could be one of the characters, who would it be (and why)?

- Would you or wouldn't you recommend this book to a friend (and why)?

- What is the most important thing about this book?

- Would you change the ending? If not, what makes it work? If yes, what changes would you make?

- If you could have a conversation with the writer, what would you say or ask?

Strategies for Inclusion

Each set of activities has been developed to meet special student interests, abilities, and learning styles. Because the questions and activities in this Study Guide are directed to the students, there are no labels to indicate the types of learners they target. However, in each Before You Read, Choices, and Book Projects page, you will find activities to meet the needs of

- *less proficient readers*
- *students acquiring English*
- *advanced students*

The activities and projects have been prepared to accommodate these different learning styles:

- *auditory/musical*
- *interpersonal*
- *intrapersonal*
- *kinesthetic*
- *logical/mathematical*
- *verbal/linguistic*
- *visual/spatial*

Using the Study Guide Questions and Activities

Encourage students to adapt the suggestions given in the Study Guide to fit their own learning styles and interests. It is important to remember that students are full of surprises, and a question or activity that is challenging to an advanced student can also be handled successfully by students who are less proficient readers. The high interest level, flexibility, and variety of these questions and activities make them appropriate for a range of students.

Students should be encouraged to vary the types of activities they choose so that the same student is not regularly selecting writing or researching activities over those involving speaking, art, and performing, and vice versa. Individual and group work should also alternate, so that students have the opportunity to work on their own and as part of collaborative learning groups.

Working in Pairs and Groups

When students with varying abilities, cultural backgrounds, and learning styles work together, they can arrive at a deeper understanding of both the book and one another.

Reading pairs can stop and check each other's responses to the book at frequent intervals.

Students from different cultural groups can interview one another about how certain situations, character interactions, character motivations, and so on would be viewed in their home cultures.

Visualizing and Performing

Students who have difficulty with writing or with presenting their ideas orally can demonstrate their understanding of the book in a variety of ways:

- making cluster diagrams or sketching their ideas
- creating tableaux showing where characters are in relation to one another during a scene, their poses or stances, and their facial expressions
- creating thought balloons with drawings or phrases that show what a character is thinking at a given moment
- drawing their own thoughts in thought balloons above a sketched self-portrait
- listing or drawing images that come to mind as they read or hear a certain section or passage of the book
- making a comic-book version of the book (with or without words)
- coming to class as a character in the book

Assessment Options

Perhaps the most important goal of assessment is to inform instruction. As you monitor the degree to which your students understand and engage with the book, you will naturally modify your instructional plan. The frequency and balance of class and small-group discussion, the time allowed for activities, and the extent to which direct teaching of reading skills and strategies, literary elements, or vocabulary is appropriate can all be planned on the basis of your ongoing assessment of your students' needs.

Several forms of assessment are particularly appropriate for work with the book:

Observing and note taking Anecdotal records that reflect both the degree and the quality of students' participation in class and small-group discussions and activities will help you target areas in which coaching or intervention is appropriate. Because communication skills are such an integral part of working with the book in a classroom setting, it is appropriate to evaluate the process of making meaning in this social context.

Involving yourself with dialogue journals and letters You may want to exchange notes with students instead of, or in addition to, encouraging them to keep reader's logs. A powerful advantage of this strategy is that at the same time you have the opportunity to evaluate students' responses, you can make a significant difference in the quality of the response. When students are aware that their comments are valued (and addressed to a real audience, an audience that writes back), they often wake up to the significance of what they are reading and begin to make stronger connections between the text and their own lives.

Agreeing on criteria for evaluation If evaluation is to be fair, it must be predictable. As students propose and plan an activity or project, collaborate with them to set up the criteria by which their work will be evaluated, and be consistent in applying only those criteria.

Encouraging self-evaluation and goal setting When students are partners with you in creating criteria for evaluation, they can apply those criteria to their own work. You might ask them to rate themselves on a simple scale of 1, 2, or 3 for each of the criteria and to arrive at an overall score. Students can then set goals based on self-evaluation.

Peer evaluation Students can participate in evaluating one another's demonstrations and presentations, basing their evaluations upon a previously established set of standards. Modeling a peer-evaluation session will help students learn this method, and a chart or checklist can guide peer discussion. Encourage students to be objective, sensitive, courteous, and constructive in their comments.

Keeping portfolios If you are in an environment where portfolios contain only carefully chosen samples of students' writing, you may want to introduce a second, "working," portfolio and negotiate grades with students after examining all or selected items from these portfolios.

Opportunities for Assessment

The suggestions in this Study Guide provide multiple opportunities for assessment across a range of skills:

- demonstrating reading comprehension
- keeping reader's logs
- listening and speaking
- working in groups—both discussion and activity-oriented
- planning, developing, and presenting a final project
- acquiring vocabulary
- taking tests

Questions for Self-evaluation and Goal Setting

- What are the three most important things I learned in my work with this book?
- How will I follow up with these so that I remember them?
- What was the most difficult part of working with this book?
- How did I deal with the difficulty, and what would I do differently?
- What two goals will I work toward in my [reading/writing/group work, etc.]?
- What steps will I take to achieve those goals?

Items for a "Working" Portfolio

- reading records
- drafts of written work and project plans
- audio- and videotapes of presentations
- notes on discussions
- reminders of cooperative projects, such as planning and discussion notes
- artwork
- objects and mementos connected with themes and topics in the book
- other evidence of engagement with the book

For help with establishing and maintaining portfolio assessment, examine the **Portfolio Management System** *in* **Elements of Literature.**

Also by the Writers

Continental Drift. New York: Knopf, 1978. Set in earthquake-threatened northern California, this book by James D. Houston focuses on a son's return from military service in Vietnam.

Don't Cry, It's Only Thunder. New York: Doubleday, 1984. Jeanne Wakatsuki Houston wrote this collection of Vietnamese personal narratives and social work case studies with Paul G. Hensler.

In the Ring of Fire: A Pacific Basin Journey. San Francisco: Mercury House, 1997. James D. Houston describes his travel and interactions in the Pacific Islands.

One Can Think About Life After the Fish Is in the Canoe

Beyond Manzanar: Views of Asian-American Womanhood

Santa Barbara, CA: Capra Press, 1985. These two works are bound together. The first is by James D. Houston; the second, by Jeanne Wakatsuki Houston.

A combined biography of Jeanne Wakatsuki Houston and James D. Houston appears in Farewell to Manzanar, *HRW Library edition. You may wish to share the following additional information with your students.*

Jeanne Wakatsuki Houston and James D. Houston have written several books. Jeanne Wakatsuki Houston is best known for *Farewell to Manzanar,* the story of her years at a World War II internment camp. To write it, she sifted through the events that she remembered, carefully recording every detail on tape. Then, she sent blank tapes to her brothers and sisters, urging them to add their own memories.

Her most important written record was a 1944 yearbook from Manzanar High School. The tapes and the yearbook awakened enough memories for a book, which she and her husband wrote together. *Farewell to Manzanar* was published in 1973, and the NBC-TV movie followed soon afterward.

Jeanne Wakatsuki Houston also is known for her essays and stories about growing up as a child of Japanese immigrants. These shorter works appear in many anthologies, among which are Laurence Yep's *American Dragons: Twenty-Five Asian American Voices* and Sylvia Watanabe's *Into the Fire: Asian American Prose.*

James D. Houston, a native of San Francisco, writes and teaches fiction at the University of California at Santa Cruz. He met Jeanne Wakatsuki when she was a student at San Jose State College. In addition to their joint work on *Farewell to Manzanar,* James D. Houston has written fifteen books of his own.

About the Book

Farewell to Manzanar is a memoir of a Japanese American family's years behind the barbed wire of a World War II internment camp. Jeanne Wakatsuki Houston, the youngest of ten children, describes the ways in which family members cope with their imprisonment. Her older brother Woody, for example, is a cheerful person who helps hold the family together by the force of his upbeat personality. Mama, in contrast, suffers mostly in silence, paying for her strength with painful knots of stress in her back. Yet it is she, and not her husband, who earns top money (by camp standards) as a camp dietician and who later becomes the family's sole wage earner.

Papa Wakatsuki dominates the family, not only by his role as head of the family, but also by his violent outbursts brought on by bouts of drinking and depression.

In some ways, Jeanne has more problems adjusting to life after her family leaves Manzanar. It takes her many years to accept herself. One reviewer summarizes Jeanne's postwar years:

> The author was growing into a world of ugly reality, where she would become aware for the first time of who she was and why she was this way. The fact she was an attractive and outgoing teenager was not enough to normalize her image. Her skin color and slanted eyes told everyone all they needed to know, and for this she grew to be ashamed.*

CRITICAL COMMENT

Farewell to Manzanar was the first book, according to one reviewer, to break through the stereotyped previous depictions of the internees:

> Now . . . Jeanne Wakatsuki Houston and James D. Houston demand recognition of politely forgotten and intentionally overlooked perspectives of camp life. . . . The accused and the humiliated internees voice the human experience of relocation and its aftermath. . . . their battles are individual and unique.
>
> —Joanne Harumi Sechi

Library Journal calls *Farewell to Manzanar* "a beautiful and very personal book." Writer Wallace Stegner calls it "A wonderful, human, feeling book . . . touching, funny, affectionate, sad, eager, and forgiving."

*"Cultural Conflicts." *Japanese in America;* page 8. Online. 22 June 1998. Available http://ssdl.cas.pacificu.edu/as/students/lwash/lori.html

For Viewing

Farewell to Manzanar. Made for TV, 1976. Well-received film of the book, whose screenplay was written by the book's coauthors.

For Listening

Farewell to Manzanar: A True Story of Japanese Experience during and after the World War II Internment. Books on Cassette, 1973. One-cassette audiobook, read by Catherine Byers.

Farewell to Manzanar. Audio Literature, 1995. Abridgment, read by Wendy Tokuda.

Copyright © by Holt, Rinehart and Winston. All rights reserved.

Make a Connection

Discuss with students the decision to send Japanese Americans away from their homes, their neighborhoods, and their jobs. At the time, why was it felt to be the right thing to do? How do students feel about the decision?

Plot

Foreword–Chapter 5   After a review of the circumstances leading up to the writing of *Farewell to Manzanar,* the story begins. When Japanese planes bomb Pearl Harbor in 1941, seven-year-old, American-born Jeanne Wakatsuki cannot grasp the significance of what has happened. Before long, however, her father is falsely accused of aiding the enemy, arrested, and sent to a detention camp in Fort Lincoln, North Dakota. Within weeks, the other family members are sent to Manzanar, a camp in the high California desert. Their homes are flimsy tarpaper shacks, stifling in summer and freezing in winter.

Chapters 6–11   Papa's arrival at Manzanar initiates a flashback describing his early life in Japan, his marriage, his many jobs, and his search for happiness. "The good life," though, escapes him again and again, and he comes to the camp a changed man. He begins drinking heavily and seldom leaves his small room.

Papa's interview with a worker at the North Dakota camp depicts an intelligent man, loyal to his adopted country. His grasp of English, however, and his early return from North Dakota suggest to many internees that he is an informer.

No sooner is a short-lived riot put down than another issue arises. The adults are asked to sign a loyalty oath and to state whether they would be willing to join the armed forces. The implications of positive and negative responses are widely debated. Eventually, Papa and Woody decide to say yes to both items.

Chapters 12–18   Slowly, life at Manzanar begins to improve, and the camp becomes more of a community. Parks are built and gardens are planted; an elementary school and a high school are built. The government begins a full-scale recreation program, bringing the Boy Scouts, glee clubs, sports leagues, movies, and traveling shows to the camp. The Wakatsukis move into a larger barracks.

Suddenly, it is 1944. Woody is drafted and leaves the camp. Shortly afterward, the internees learn that their evacuation orders have been overturned in court and that Manzanar is slated to be closed. In June 1945, the camp schools close, never to reopen. In August, the bombing of Hiroshima ends the war in the Pacific.

The news that the camp is closing is not good for Jeanne's family. They have no money, no work, and no home. Papa worries at every departure, knowing that his turn is coming. By October, only the old, the soldiers' wives, and the very young remain at Manzanar.

Chapters 19–22 In October 1945, the Wakatsukis leave Manzanar for Long Beach, California. There they find an apartment, and Mama goes to work in a cannery. Papa stays at home; to him, such work is undignified.

Jeanne does well in school but is puzzled at people's attitudes toward her. Some see only her Japanese face; others ignore her. Longing to be accepted, Jeanne becomes a junior high baton twirler and leader of the drum majorettes for a Boy Scout drum and bugle corps. She goes on to be a majorette at her high school.

By Jeanne's senior year, Papa has gone back to farming, and Jeanne achieves a dream: becoming the annual carnival queen. Jeanne graduates from college, marries, and has a family. In 1972, she returns to Manzanar, an uninhabited desert once more. There, in the chill wind from the Sierras, she comes to terms with her time there and finds a sense of peace.

Plot Elements: While this book is not a novel with a plot constructed by the writer, the story has many elements of a conventional plot: conflict, resolution, rising action, climax, denouement. (See below for a more complete treatment of the plot devices of conflict and flashback.)

Theme

Students will see the following **themes** developed in detail in *Farewell to Manzanar.*

The Importance of Heritage Especially in the **flashbacks** and asides, the writers show how Papa is driven by his samurai background and how this background contributes to his feeling crushed each time circumstance turns against him. On the other hand, they show the depth of Woody's happiness when he visits Hiroshima and discovers Papa's family home. Through these devices, as well as through Jeanne's **internal conflicts,** readers see the power of both cultural tradition and family history in shaping the lives of the Wakatsuki family.

Make a Connection

Have students spend a few minutes freewriting about the word *prejudice.* Have them refer to their notes as you discuss how it feels to be the target of prejudice.

Connecting with *Elements of Literature*

You can use *Farewell to Manzanar* to extend students' examination of the themes and topics presented in *Elements of Literature.*

- Introductory Course : "Justice for All," Collection Five
- First Course: "Who Am I?" Collection Two
- Second Course: "From Generation to Generation," Collection Two

The Power of Prejudice   During and after World War II, prejudice against Japanese Americans was commonplace, especially in California. As they prepare for internment, the Wakatsukis are besieged by secondhand dealers who offer insulting prices for family treasures. The accommodations at Manzanar cover only the bare necessities, and the Japanese Americans are insulted again by their lack of privacy. Even when the Wakatsukis return to the outside world, the prejudice continues. Mama takes a menial job, all she is offered, and Jeanne is refused admission to the Girl Scouts. For Jeanne, the worst part of prejudice is her feeling that being shunned and uninvited is somehow her own fault.

Self-Discovery   Jeanne is the focus of the story, and we see much growth in her as the plot unfolds. At first she is a victim—a target of Executive Order 9066, an unwilling resident of Manzanar, and a witness to her father's abuses. Once the family is released, however, Jeanne is older and keenly aware of her need for an identity. Although she tries to forge a persona like that of the Caucasian girls with whom she goes to school, she still faces **conflicts** within herself and with her family. In time, Jeanne discovers her own identity and is able to incorporate the difficult experiences of her childhood into her personality as an adult.

Make a Connection

Point out that Jeanne is both a real person and a **character** in a story. Call on volunteers to share their thoughts about what that might mean to the way that we as readers react to the story.

Characters

Students will meet the following major **characters** in *Farewell to Manzanar.*

Jeanne Wakatsuki Houston is the focus of this true story, and all of the events and other characters are seen through her eyes. During the course of the narrative, she grows from a seven-year-old child to an adult.

Papa is Ko Wakatsuki, Jeanne's father. The experience of internment changes him dramatically as he loses his home and his ability to support his family.

Mama is Riku Wakatsuki, who bears most of the weight of caring for her large family in the Manzanar years.

Woody, one of Jeanne's older brothers, keeps the family together, especially during their first few days at Manzanar.

Kiyo, another brother (a few years older than Jeanne), finds the courage to stop Papa from seriously harming Mama.

The Catholic nuns inside Manzanar help Jeanne feel accepted and consider her a part of their small world.

Radine befriends Jeanne from sixth grade through junior high but drifts away in high school.

Setting

This book is the story of a setting and of the short- and long-term effects of that setting on the people who experienced it. The World War II environment and the internment situation are the major elements of the setting. Manzanar, the relocation camp that lies in the high desert of California, is a wild place of subzero winters and blazing summers. The Wakatsuki family, accustomed to the benign climate of Southern California, struggles daily against the widely fluctuating temperatures, the sandstorms, and the soft gray dust that filters through wall cracks and floorboards throughout the camp.

As difficult as Manzanar is, the postwar outside world, where the last part of the story takes place, presents enormous problems for the family. It is a place where Jeanne suffers rejection, apathy, feelings of invisibility, and the sense that no matter what she does, she never can be part of the American scene. Toward the end of the story, the setting progresses into the writers' present world and the visit to the site of Manzanar that has such a profound effect on Jeanne.

Point of View

To tell the story of Manzanar, the writers use several different points of view. The **first-person point of view** dominates. Readers see only what Jeanne sees, hear only what she hears, and so on. **Characters** enter and depart only as their lives connect with her own.

Flashbacks and asides use a **third-person point of view** to depict scenes at which the narrator was not present.

Make a Connection

To help students understand the critical importance of setting, ask them to imagine their lives in a completely different place and write three ways their lives would be different.

*A **Literary Elements Worksheet** that focuses on setting appears on page 40 of this Study Guide.*

Make a Connection

Discuss with students the ways in which **point of view** can change how readers understand a **scene** or situation. Encourage students to give examples, such as changing the point of view of an adventure story from the hero's to the villain's.

Key Elements *(continued)*

Make a Connection ▌

Have students name a film, book, or television program with which they all are familiar. Discuss its external and internal conflicts. What are the signals that conflict is present? Encourage students to apply those clues to their reading of *Farewell to Manzanar.*

A *Literary Elements Worksheet* that focuses on conflict appears on page 41 of this Study Guide.

Conflict

A story's **conflicts** lie in struggles between opposing **characters** or forces. In this story, the external conflicts are, first of all, those between the American government and its own Japanese American residents and citizens. Conflicts arise between different factions in the camp. The family members sometimes clash with one another and with various other internees. Some characters face **internal conflict,** as well, and they struggle within themselves. Papa, for example, tries hard to overcome his circumstances but fails again and again. After Manzanar, Jeanne struggles against both prejudice and her unreachable goal of fitting seamlessly into the culture around her.

Make a Connection ▌

A *Literary Elements Worksheet* that focuses on flashback appears on page 42 of this Study Guide.

Flashback

Flashbacks and asides occur throughout *Farewell to Manzanar.* The most important flashback occurs in Chapter Six, which deals with Papa's early life, his courtship of Mama, and their family life before the internment. This flashback provides insights into Papa's personality and his later actions. One significant aside is an episode in which a Wakatsuki son reestablishes ties with family members back in Japan. Both flashbacks and asides give greater depth to the story as a whole and provide a basis for interpreting the family's responses to internment and its aftermath.

Before You Read

Activities

BUILDING ON PRIOR KNOWLEDGE

Meet Manzanar

Berlin. Pearl Harbor. Auschwitz. Hiroshima. You probably recognize these place names in connection with World War II, but have you ever heard of a place called Manzanar? Look up the name in a few reference books or on the Internet. Find out what Manzanar was; then, share the information. What is your reaction to knowing that such places existed in the United States at that time? Why?

MAKING PERSONAL CONNECTIONS

Continuity in a Changing Land

Almost no country in the world has the variety of cultures that the United States has. What culture or cultures are part of your heritage? What traditions or foods of that culture are a part of your life? Quickwrite about aspects of your cultural heritage. (This activity can be private; you need not share it with others.)

REFLECTING

H-O-M-E

How would you feel if you were suddenly forced to move away from your familiar surroundings? What would you miss about your town? about your school? about your friends? Through writing, drawing, or collecting photographs, show what you would miss. If you decide to share what you create, you might want to work with other students to put together a bulletin board showing the things you value and would miss about your current life.

Story Notes

Use **Story Notes, Issue 1**

- to find out more about some of the topics and themes in *Farewell to Manzanar*
- to get ideas for writing activities and projects that will take you deeper into the book

Making Meanings

First Thoughts

1. What is your reaction to the way the Japanese American families are treated?

Shaping Interpretations

2. Compare Jeanne's reaction to her father's being sent away to her reaction when she sees him again. Why are her feelings so different?

3. **Irony** is a contrast between what we expect to happen and what actually happens. What is ironic about the threat that Jeanne and Kiyo face from students at Terminal Island?

4. When the family is given forty-eight hours to leave Terminal Island, Mama destroys her porcelain dinner set. Why?

5. Why do you think Chapter 5 is called "Almost a Family"?

Connecting with the Text

6. The internees at Manzanar work hard to make the camp a better place to live. If you had been there, what ideas for improvement might you have offered?

Extending the Text

7. "She [Mama] would quickly subordinate her own desires . . . because she knew cooperation was the only way to survive." In what other situations is cooperation necessary for survival?

Challenging the Text

8. Near the end of this section, there is a "fast-forward" to a few incidents that occur after the camps have closed. Did this shift in **setting** add to your understanding of the story? Explain.

> **READING CHECK**
>
> **a.** Why is Papa forced to leave his family? Why is the family forced to leave Terminal Island?
>
> **b.** Name three difficulties that the Wakatsukis endure during their first weeks at Manzanar.
>
> **c.** How does Woody help the family adjust to Manzanar?
>
> **d.** How does eating at the mess hall change the structure of family units?
>
> **e.** When Papa returns from North Dakota, how has he changed?

Choices: Building Your Portfolio

COOPERATIVE LEARNING

Papa's Tale

What happened to Papa in North Dakota? Why did he seem to grow old so quickly? Get together with a few classmates and suggest answers to these and other questions that you may have had about Papa as you were reading. Share your conclusions with the class and see if anyone has details to add.

CREATIVE WRITING

Official Report

Imagine that you're one of the officials in charge of Manzanar. Write a report that you might have prepared shortly after the internees arrived. Here are some things that you might include:

- your impression of the internees' feelings about the camp
- the problems that they are having, plus any solutions that they have found.
- what you could do to improve the situation.
- your predictions about how effective the relocation program will be, using Manzanar as an example

Compare reports with a partner.

CHARACTER DIARY

Dear Diary . . .

Imagine that you are Jeanne's older brother Woody, who acts as head of the family while Papa is away. Write a diary entry that he might have made during one of the family's early days at Manzanar. In character, describe some of the things that you do for the other members of your family. If you wish, compare diary entries with a classmate. How does putting yourself in the place of Jeanne's brother help you understand the story and its **characters** better?

Consider This . . .

There is a phrase the Japanese use in such situations, when something difficult must be endured. . . . "Shikata ga nai" (It cannot be helped). "Shikata ga nai" (It must be done).

Why is it sometimes better to endure a difficult situation than to fight it?

Writing Follow-up: Reflecting

Write a paragraph explaining your reactions to the meanings of the phrase *shikata ga nai* ("It cannot be helped" and "It must be done").

Story Notes

Use **Story Notes, Issue 2**

- to find out more about some of the topics and themes in this section of the book
- to get ideas for writing activities and other projects related to *Farewell to Manzanar*

Making Meanings

First Thoughts

1. Were you surprised that Papa decided to go to the meeting? Explain why or why not.

Shaping Interpretations

2. How does Papa's early life show how much he valued pride and dignity?

3. At the end of Chapter 7, Papa asks his interviewer, "When your mother and your father are having a fight, do you want them to kill each other? Or do you just want them to stop fighting?" What does he mean?

READING CHECK

a. From what kinds of families do Jeanne's parents come? How do Papa and Mama manage to get married?

b. How do Papa and Mama celebrate their twenty-fifth wedding anniversary?

c. What does the Japanese word *inu* mean?

d. How does Kiyo keep Papa from beating Mama when he hears about the *inu* insult?

e. What request from the government causes great debate in the camp?

4. Just after the December Riot, the mess hall bells ring. The ringing continues until noon the next day. In your opinion, what is the purpose of the ringing?

5. How does the aside about Kaz at the reservoir shack illustrate the tensions between the internees and the camp personnel?

6. The end of Chapter 11 also brings Part 1 of Jeanne's story to an end. What conflicts are represented in the last scene?

Connecting with the Text

7. Re-read the oath that appears at the beginning of Chapter 11. Would you have signed it? Why or why not?

Extending the Text

8. Her parents' silver wedding anniversary was a significant event for Jeanne. Why are celebrations of events in their lives important to people?

Challenging the Text

9. Do you think that the **flashback** about Papa's and Mama's early lives is important to the narrative? Explain your answer.

Choices: Building Your Portfolio

TABLEAU

You Are There

Work with some classmates to create a tableau. Choose a key scene from this section of the book and "freeze" it in place. Then, one student at a time "unfreezes" and speaks in character. The student should explain what the character is thinking during the scene. Feel free to include gestures, postures, and facial expressions to express the characters' personalities. If possible, videotape the performance. Afterward, be ready to tell how it felt to be the character you portrayed and how the gestures, postures, and expressions helped you express the character's personality.

CREATIVE WRITING

Speaking from the Heart

Choose one **character** from Chapters 6–11. "Become" that person long enough to write a poem from his or her **point of view.** Follow this format, filling in the blanks below.

I am _____.

I wonder _____.

I hear _____.

I see _____.

I want _____!

I pretend _____.

I feel _____.

I worry _____.

I understand _____.

I say _____.

I dream _____.

I try _____.

I am _____!

DISCUSSION GROUP

That's Interesting!

From Chapters 6–11, choose a short passage that you found memorable. In a group, take turns reading aloud your passages and discussing the passages that you hear. Which passages were most interesting? Which were surprising or upsetting? Which expressed a thought in a unique or interesting way?

Consider This . . .

[Papa] was not a great man. He wasn't even a very successful man. He was a poser, a braggart, and a tyrant. But he had held onto his self-respect. . . .

Jeanne writes these words years after the family's stay at Manzanar. How well do you think she understood her father *during* the internment?

Writing Follow-up: Persuading ▪

Write a few paragraphs with the goal of persuading Papa that he can regain his self-respect by behaving differently.

Story Notes

Use **Story Notes, Issue 3**

- to find out more about of the topics and themes in this section of the book
- to get ideas for writing activities and other projects related to *Farewell to Manzanar*

Making Meanings

First Thoughts

1. What event in this section stood out to you? Why?

Shaping Interpretations

2. How do the pear and apple trees that Papa tends **symbolize,** or represent, what is happening in Manzanar in 1943 and 1944?

3. How does the drafting of internees change life at Manzanar?

4. Describe the **internal conflict,** or clash of thoughts and feelings, that Jeanne and others feel about the closing of the internment camps.

Connecting with the Text

5. Suppose that you could step into the book at this point and ask any of the characters a question. With whom would you speak? What would you want to know?

Extending the Text

6. Papa made a rock garden; other men built a park with ponds and waterfalls. Why are activities and places like these important to people?

Challenging the Text

7. When Woody's Japanese aunt talks to him in the dark, he touches the corner of his eye and feels wetness. His throat feels so thick that he can't speak. Why do you think the writers didn't just say that he was crying?

> **READING CHECK**
>
> Here are three important events from Chapters 12–18. Copy them onto a sheet of paper; then add at least two more events to the list. Number the events in **chronological order**—that is, the order in which they happened.
>
> - The closing of Manzanar is announced.
> - Woody visits Hiroshima.
> - Jeanne wants to be baptized as a Catholic.

Choices: Building Your Portfolio

WORKING WITH A PARTNER

Getting into Character

To check your understanding of Jeanne's story, work with a partner to prepare a brief **dialogue** between her and another character—for example, Woody, Lois, or Mama. As they talk, the characters should share their feelings about an event that took place in Chapters 12–18. Rehearse with your partner; then, share the dialogue with the class.

CREATIVE WRITING

Expert Advice

It seems that everyone in the camp has time for a hobby. Papa paints watercolors; Jeanne becomes a baton twirler. Imagine that you are at Manzanar and you want to teach other internees about one of your hobbies. Write a brochure to explain how to get started with that hobby. Begin by listing any items needed. Then, "spell out" each step in the order in which your readers should proceed. Include diagrams, if necessary. You also might want to give advice about trouble spots or explain how your readers will know that they are doing a task correctly.

MAP

Lay It Out

On your own or with a partner, draw a map of Manzanar. Include a compass rose to indicate north, south, east, and west. Remember to show the Sierras and the reservoir. Since all the barracks were similarly laid out, you need not show all of the blocks. However, be sure to in-clude the important buildings, including the camp offices, guard towers, mess halls, latrines, hospital, schools, and the "Children's Village." Display the finished map in class.

Consider This . . .

After three years in our desert ghetto, at least we knew where we stood with our neighbors, could live more or less at ease with them.

How has Manzanar become a "comfortable" place to live?

Writing Follow-up: Comparing

Write a paragraph or two comparing the living conditions in Manzanar when the Wakatsuki family arrived to the conditions at this point in the story.

Story Notes

Use **Story Notes, Issue 4**

- to find out more about of the topics and themes in Chapters 12–18
- to get ideas for writing activities and other projects related to *Farewell to Manzanar*

Farewell to Manzanar

Making Meanings

a. Why is Papa so depressed during the family's stay in Long Beach?

b. What happens to Jeanne on her first day back in a public school?

c. How do things change between Jeanne and her friend Radine when they enter high school?

d. Why does Papa finally leave Long Beach and the run-down apartment in Cabrillo Homes?

e. What two things is the adult Jeanne the first in her family to do?

First Thoughts

1. Which part of Chapters 19–22 surprised you most?

Shaping Interpretations

2. Just before leaving Manzanar, Papa shows off the car that he has just bought. What does this **scene** suggest about Papa's personality?

3. On her first day back at school, Jeanne says that she longs to be invisible. What does she mean? What opposite wish creates an **internal conflict** for her?

4. After the camp, why is Papa so often angry with Jeanne?

5. Why do the years at Manzanar become a kind of secret to Jeanne?

6. How is Jeanne affected by her return to Manzanar?

Connecting with the Text

7. As Jeanne revisits Manzanar, the scent of cork burning brings back memories of the family's last days in the camp. What memory has a certain sight, sound, or smell suddenly brought back to your mind?

Extending the Text

8. Do you think contests like the carnival queen election in this story are a good idea? Why or why not?

Challenging the Text

9. Why do you think the book ends with a story about Papa back at Manzanar? Do you find this ending effective? Explain.

Choices: Building Your Portfolio

LITERATURE GROUP

Theme Hunt

With a few classmates, form a theme-hunting group. Together, choose one of the major **themes** of *Farewell to Manzanar:* "The Importance of Heritage," "The Power of Prejudice," or "Self-Discovery." Then, take turns giving examples from this section of the story that illustrate that theme. When you have named all the examples you can, try a "hunt" on another theme.

ART

Memorial for Manzanar

What is the best kind of memorial for Manzanar and the internment program? With a partner, create a design plan for a memorial park. First, draw the memorial itself. Next, sketch the layout of the park. Finally, provide a written description of how your design memorializes the internment program. Present your design to the class and ask for their response. Would they support your choice?

CREATIVE WRITING

Going Back

Imagine yourself in thirty years revisiting the place you live now or a place you have lived in the past. Write a journal entry on what your thoughts might be.

Consider This . . .

". . . I lived with this double impulse; the urge to disappear and the desperate desire to be acceptable."

This was Jeanne's feeling when she went back to public school. Is this feeling familiar to you, too?

Writing Follow-up: Problem–Solution ■

Consider the actions Jeanne took in response to this feeling. Then write three suggestions for someone who is facing this problem. Explain each suggestion in a separate paragraph.

Story Notes

Use **Story Notes, Issue 5**

- to find out more about of the topics and themes in Chapters 19–22
- to get ideas for writing activities and other projects related to *Farewell to Manzanar*

Cross-Curricular Connections

SCIENCE

Desert Flora, Desert Fauna

What kinds of plants and animals could be found around Manzanar? Choose two or three plants and two or three animals. Do research to find out how they are suited to the desert environment, how they find food, how long they live, and so on. If you wish, work with some classmates to create a bulletin-board display to present your information.

ART

Manzanar Mural

On your own or with a partner, make a mural to show daily life at Manzanar. Try focusing on one small part of the camp, but show as many activities as possible. Here are some ideas:

- people making rock gardens or parks
- people caring for vegetable gardens
- people attending adult education classes
- a teenage dance
- baton twirling, ballet, and glee club shows
- children playing baseball

MATH

Camp Cuisine Calculations

What would it be like to buy food to serve in Manzanar's mess halls? Make up a sample menu (using items that Jeanne mentions, if you wish). Keep in mind that about ten thousand people lived at Manzanar. Figure out how much of each item you would have to buy. Turn the results into a shopping list.

SOCIAL STUDIES

One Thing Leads to Another

Research the causes and effects of the war in the Pacific. Answer these questions:

- Why did the Japanese attack Pearl Harbor?
- How did the United States respond?
- What were the major events leading to the bombing of Hiroshima?
- What effect did that bombing have on the war?

HEALTH

Dietician Data

Mama works as a dietician in Manzanar. What work do dieticians do today? Gather some facts about this career. If possible, talk to the school dietician or a dietician at a hospital in your community. (You might even ask your teacher to invite a dietician to speak to the class about his or her work.) Share your findings.

Multimedia and Internet Connections

NOTE: Check with your teacher about school policies on accessing Internet sites. If a Web site named here is unavailable, use key words to locate a similar site.

VINTAGE RECORDINGS: MUSIC

Dance Party!

Imagine that you're the DJ for a dance at Manzanar. What recordings will you play? Find at least three selections of 1940s music. (Many libraries have music collections from various eras, and there should be a good selection from the World War II years.) Play your selections for the class (dancing optional), and explain why you chose each one. Then, lead a discussion about what the music might have meant (1) to the Issei and (2) to the Nisei.

REVIEW: FILM

Other Views of Internment

With your teacher's help, view one or two of the following films. Afterward, compare the experiences in *Farewell to Manzanar* with those in the film.

- **Guilty By Reason of Race** (55 min.): This NBC-TV documentary uses still photographs, interviews, and newsreel footage to document the internment era. (Contact any of these university film libraries for rental information: Alaska, Arizona State, Colorado, Florida State, Georgia, Iowa, Illinois, Indiana, Kent State, Michigan, Minnesota, Nebraska, New Hampshire, North Carolina, Oregon State, Pennsylvania, South Carolina, South Dakota State, Utah, Central Washington State, and Wisconsin.)

- **Nisei: The Pride and the Shame** (55 min.): This CBS-TV documentary is narrated by Walter Cronkite. It can be rented from the Japanese American Citizens League, 1765 Sutter Street, San Francisco, CA 94115.

- **Manzanar** (16 min.): This is an award-winning color documentary by Robert Nakamura. It uses both live action and stills to capture a young boy's years at Manzanar. It can be rented from Visual Communications, 125 Weller Street, Room 312, Los Angeles, CA 90012.

RESEARCH: INTERNET

Visit Manzanar!

You can visit Manzanar via the World Wide Web. Many Internet sites deal with the Japanese American internment. Use the key word *Manzanar* to search on your own, or explore one of these sites:

- http://www.qnet.com/~earthsun/remember.htm
  Here you can find information on the Manzanar National Historic Site.

- http://www.nps.gov/manz
  Here you can learn about the annual Manzanar Pilgrimage.

- http://www.umass.edu/history/internment.html
  This is a gallery of photographs about the internment era.

Create a presentation of new information you found that adds to your understanding of the experiences in *Farewell to Manzanar.*

Making Meanings

Story Notes
See *Issue 6*

1. In what ways are the writer's experiences most like yours?

2. What is the high point for the writer of her family's cross-country trip?

3. What does the writer realize when she receives the compliment in Connecticut?

4. What does Uchida mean by saying that she learned "a lot of Japanese by osmosis"?

5. **Onomatopoeia** is the use of words whose sounds imitate their meaning. How does Uchida's mother use onomatopoeia to create new words?

6. Compare this writer's experience to Jeanne Wakatsuki's. How are they alike?

7. The writer didn't understand her mother's doll collection until she was "older and wiser." What things do people in your family value that you may not appreciate until you, too, are older and wiser?

READING CHECK

Make a word web. Place Uchida's name in the center of a circle. Around this circle, draw several smaller circles that have lines connecting to the center circle. In these circles, write some of the things that Yoshiko Uchida thought were difficult about being Japanese American.

Making Meanings

Executive Order 9066

Story Notes
See **Issue 7**

1. In your own words, summarize this document. What is your reaction to it—and why?

2. What is meant by *military area?* Why would a military area be important?

3. How will this order be enforced? How do you know?

4. What arrangements are made for those who are to be "excluded" from military areas? In your opinion, why doesn't the order go into detail?

5. From your reading of *Farewell to Manzanar,* would you say that Executive Order 9066 was an effective document? Explain. Do you think something like this should be done again in an emergency situation? Why or why not?

> **READING CHECK**
>
> **a.** Who issues Executive Order 9066?
>
> **b.** How much time has passed between the bombing of Pearl Harbor and the issuing of this document?
>
> **c.** According to the text, who has the responsibility of providing food and shelter for the internees?

Apology, Payment 48 Years in Making

Story Notes
See **Issue 7**

1. What do you think of the government's gesture? In your opinion, is the repayment adequate? Explain.

2. What details in the news story confirm or support events that you have read about in *Farewell to Manzanar?*

3. Do you find anything **ironic** about the payments that the elderly Japanese Americans receive? Explain.

4. Why do you think so many people don't remember, know about, or understand what happened to people of Japanese ancestry during World War II?

5. Do you think the government should do anything else for the Japanese Americans who were relocated? Does it matter that the evacuation happened so many years ago? Explain.

> **READING CHECK**
>
> **a.** How much money does Teru Noda receive from the United States government?
>
> **b.** Who has sent a letter along with that money?
>
> **c.** What happened to Shigeo Tanaka's farm while he was interned at Manzanar?

Making Meanings

Photograph of a Child, Destination: Tule Lake Relocation Center

Story Notes
See *Issue 7*

1. The **titles** of the two poems refer to journeys that the child and the woman must take. For which of them do you feel more sympathy? Explain.

2. In "Photograph of a Child," what details did the writer probably see in the photograph? What details could not have appeared in the photograph?

READING CHECK

a. In "Photograph of a Child," why is the child on a pier?

b. In "Destination: Tule Lake Relocation Center," what has the woman managed to take with her?

3. What is the significance of the two things the child in "Photograph of a Child" is holding?

4. What is meant by these lines in "Destination: Tule Lake"?

> wiping
> sight back with a wrinkled
> hand-
> kerchief. . . .

5. In "Destination: Tule Lake," why does the woman *worry* the strings of a baggage tag? What definition of *worry* fits the situation in the poem?

Story Notes

INTRODUCING *Farewell to Manzanar*

History in a Nutshell

Japanese Americans in World War II

In the first few months following Pearl Harbor, the Japanese military seriously damaged the U.S. Pacific fleet and swiftly captured a series of islands. To many observers, it seemed clear that Japan was planning an invasion of the West Coast of the United States.

In this environment of fear, a general suspicion of Japanese Americans began to grow in the U.S. Some politicians and journalists publicly stated that they suspected Japanese Americans on the West Coast of spying for the Japanese military. Acts of discrimination increased, and many banks, grocers, and other businesses refused to do business with people of Japanese ancestry.

Only two months after the U.S. entered the war, President Roosevelt signed Executive Order 9066, which allowed U.S. military leaders to evacuate anyone they thought might pose a threat to the security of the United States.

Very quickly, more than 110,000 people of Japanese ancestry—virtually the entire Japanese community in the West—were forced out of their homes. Most of these dislocated people were moved into camps, where they were confined behind barbed wire fences and guarded by Army police. After two years, the internees were finally allowed to return to their homes—or what was left of them.

FOR YOUR READER'S LOG

The title of *Farewell to Manzanar* refers to saying goodbye to a place and to a part of one's life. To what places or people have you had to say goodbye?

WHO WERE THEY?

The Japanese Americans who were forced into internment camps had been engaged in many occupations. Here are just a few:

Disney animators	sales workers
teachers	gardeners
doctors	cooks
dentists	waiters
engineers	farmers
judges	barbers
lawyers	beauticians
pharmacists	photographers
hotel managers	ship captains

Story Notes

Farewell to Manzanar FOREWORD–CHAPTER 5

Japanese Americans Cooperate to Prove Loyalty

One spokesperson for the Japanese American community was Mike Masaoka, national secretary of the Japanese American Citizens League. He wrote in the *Japanese American Courier* that while internment would be the hardest fight the Japanese American people would probably ever face, they would show the world that they were exemplary citizens.

The JACL president agreed. He announced that Japanese Americans would willingly "go into exile." They were cooperating, he said, because it was a way of showing loyalty to the U.S.

FOR YOUR READER'S LOG

If you had been an internee, which aspects of Manzanar would you have found most frustrating?

What's in a Name?

The members of Jeanne Wakatsuki Houston's immediate family were named after a dazzling array of famous Americans.

- Houston's father Ko took the personal name George in honor of George Washington.
- Her mother Riku took the name Martha for Martha Washington.

- Woody was named for former president Woodrow Wilson.
- Jeanne was named after U.S. movie star Jean Harlow.

Ray's name, however, was simply an American version of his Japanese name, Reijiro.

The Word PLACE

Allusions

An allusion is a reference to something or someone—from literature, history, or another field—with which many people are familiar. In *Farewell to Manzanar,* the writers make several allusions.

armada: This is a reference to the Spanish Armada, a huge fleet of ships that fought the English

(and lost) in 1588. The fleet of fishing boats that left Terminal Island and suddenly returned looked like an armada to Jeanne.

Charlie Chaplins: This is a reference to the famous silent film star Charlie Chaplin, who, as part of his comedy routines, often wore mismatched clothing much too large for him, like the camp clothing.

kabuki creatures: This is a reference to the actors in Kabuki, a

form of Japanese theater, who powder their faces white and often have deep, V-shaped "widow's peak" hairlines. The nurses Jeanne saw in the clinic had adopted the Kabuki look.

Story Notes

Issue 3

Farewell to Manzanar CHAPTERS 6–11

A Samurai Heritage

Ko Wakatsuki came from a long line of *samurai*. The samurai were a class of fierce warriors, legendary for their courage, their code of unquestioning loyalty and obedience, and their sense of personal honor. The samurai are famous for their choice of suicide over dishonor.

Many samurai families clung to their class and privileges well into the twentieth century.

FOR YOUR READER'S LOG

The Manzanar riot was at least partly due to the internees' anger and frustration at being confined. What do you think might have been done to make conditions at the camp better?

Camps Develop Within the Camp

At Manzanar, conflict developed between two factions: a group of older internees who were active in the camp labor unions and the younger, mostly college-educated members of the Japanese American Citizens League.

JACL members believed that it was important for the survival of the internees to work harmoniously with the camp administration. The union leaders, on the other hand, believed in active protest, and some union members suspected members of the JACL of being informants.

ASK the Professor

Dear Dr. I. Knoweverything,

My family visited the site of the Manzanar camp last August, and it was really hot! Was the weather that miserable at all the camps?

—**Temperate in Tacoma**

Dear Temperate,

The barracks didn't provide much shelter—some of them were made mostly of tar paper. Most of the camps were extremely hot in the summer and quite cold in the winter, and there wasn't much the internees could do about it.

The hottest camp was Poston in the Arizona desert. Poston had three separate units, officially named Poston I, Poston II, and Poston III, but the internees renamed them *Poston, Toastin', and Roastin'*.

Story Notes

Farewell to Manzanar CHAPTERS 12–18

"Don't Fence Me In"

The music that was popular in the early 1940s included the big dance bands led by Benny Goodman, Duke Ellington, Glenn Miller, Artie Shaw, and others. Teenagers at Manzanar probably jitterbugged to "In the Mood" and "Take the A Train" and slowdanced to music like "Begin the Beguine," "Stardust," and "Moonglow."

The war gave rise to songs like "Don't Sit Under the Apple Tree" and "I'll Get By." The Andrews Sisters became immensely popular for such upbeat tunes as "Mairsy Doats" and "The Boogie Woogie Bugle Boy of Company B."

Western, or cowboy, music also grew popular during the forties. Cowboy singers Gene Autry and Roy Rogers became famous for songs like "Home on the Range," "Drifting Along with the Tumbling Tumbleweeds," and "Don't Fence Me In"—which was especially popular at Manzanar.

Poetry in the Camps

Poetry clubs sprang up in many camps, including Manzanar. Here are two poems from the camps:*

Fortunate me; Indifferent
To the fierce fighting
All over the world,
Here I am, learning
Flower arrangement, writing, and
embroidery.

The cream of the crop—
Nisei soldiers—raised
By wrinkles on the parents' brow.

*From *Democracy on Trial* by Page Smith. Copyright © 1995 by Page Smith. Reprinted by permission of **Simon & Schuster.**

FOR YOUR READER'S LOG

In 1944, the U.S. government began quietly sending selected internees back to areas on the California coast. If your family had been one of the groups selected, would you have wanted to go or not? As you read Chapters 12–18, make some notes in a two-column chart. In the left hand column, record the things you might have feared about re-entering society. In the right-hand column, jot down the things to which you might have looked forward.

Story Notes

Farewell to Manzanar CHAPTERS 19–22

Nisei Unit Most Decorated in U.S. Army

Many young men at Manzanar and the other camps enlisted voluntarily in the U.S. military from 1943 on. Most served in segregated units in Europe under extremely harsh conditions.

One of the best-known Nisei units was the 442nd Combat Team, which was made up mostly of former internees. By the end of the war, the 442nd was the most decorated unit in the entire U.S. Army, earning 3,600 Purple Hearts, 810 Bronze Stars, 342 Silver Stars, 47 Distinguished Service Crosses, 17 Legions of Merit, and hundreds of other medals.

As news spread of the bravery of the Nisei soldiers, the casualties they suffered, and the medals they won, the anti-Japanese voices in America gradually quieted. By the fall of 1944, speaking out against Japanese Americans was no longer as acceptable as it had been two years before.

☆ ☆

New Lives After Camp

When the internment camps finally closed, the lives of the women internees had changed. Before the evacuation, most of them had spent their time cooking, cleaning, and caring for the children.

In the camps, however, many children were separated from their parents, and child care and cooking were both taken over by the camp administration. Suddenly, the interned women had time on their hands. Some attended classes and studied English and other subjects.

When the camps closed, many of the women internees were qualified for careers they might not have considered before the war. Many took jobs as teachers, dietitians, nurses, or salespeople. Of all the tremendous changes brought about by the evacuation, the transformation of the interned women from homemakers to wage earners may have been the greatest.

FOR YOUR READER'S LOG

If you were the son or daughter—or grandson or granddaughter—of someone who had lived at Manzanar, how would you feel about the run-down state of this historic site? As you read the end of *Farewell to Manzanar* (especially Chapter 22), jot down any ideas you have about how the site could be made into a more fitting memorial.

Manzanar Today

What's left of the Manzanar camp stands just off Highway 395 near Lone Pine, California. Not much is left besides the sentry posts, the old auditorium, and the camp cemetery. Yet Manzanar is a National Historic Site—a memorial to remind future generations that once 10,000 people were confined there.

Small groups of former residents still visit Manzanar once a year. On the last Saturday in April they gather to remember the internees who lived there not really so long ago.

Story Notes

Farewell to Manzanar CONNECTIONS

• JAPANESE AMERICAN WRITERS •
Yoshiko Uchida

Born in California in 1922, Yoshiko Uchida started writing early in her life. At ten years old, she was already writing short stories in handmade brown paper books. Most of Uchida's early works were written for and about young people in Japan. That changed, however, when she wrote *Journey to Topaz,* the story of her family's years in a relocation camp in Utah.

Journey to Topaz and most of Uchida's later works deal with the experiences of Japanese Americans. *The Invisible Thread,* from which this Connections piece is taken, tells of Uchida's family life before, during, and after the forced relocation. "I hope to give young Asian-Americans a sense of their past and to reinforce their self-esteem and self-knowledge," Uchida says.*

Connections

• **Chapter Three from**
The Invisible Thread

The Doll Festival of Hinamatsuri

Originally the dolls displayed during Hinamatsuri were simple straw figures. The traditional belief was that if the figures were floated downstream in a river, bad luck would go along with them. Today, the dolls are heirlooms, passed down from mother to daughter over the generations. The festival lasts for one to two weeks. Then, the dolls are quickly put away until the following year. No one plays with these dolls in the time between festivals because the dolls are delicate and expensive—and because an old superstition says it would bring bad luck.

FOR YOUR READER'S LOG

As you read about Uchida's memories, note the ways in which she as a child was somewhat like you or your friends. Also note the things that were different. What can you learn from the comparison?

JAPANESE FOLK TALES: "The Tongue-Cut Sparrow"

"The Tongue-Cut Sparrow" is one of the many Japanese folk tales Yoshiko Uchida learned from her mother.

The tongue-cut sparrow was the pet of an old man. When the bird innocently angered the man's wife, she cut off part of its tongue and sent the sparrow away. The man finally found the sparrow and its family and stayed with them for a time. When he was about to leave and return home, he was rewarded with a basket full of gold and silver.

When the man's wife saw the treasure, she, too, decided to visit the sparrow. The sparrow was not happy to see her but allowed her to stay with its family for a while. As she prepared to leave, the bird gave her a choice of two baskets, one heavy and one light. She chose the heavy basket, thinking it would be full of silver and gold. However, when she opened it on her way home, she was horrified to find it was filled with goblins and elves.

*From **Contemporary Authors,** 1997. Published by Gale Research, New York.

Story Notes

Issue 7

Farewell to Manzanar CONNECTIONS

Editor Defends His Neighbors

After the bombing of Pearl Harbor, Lowell Pratt, the editor of the Selma, California newspaper, supported his Japanese American neighbors. On March 5, 1942, he wrote,

> Many [Japanese Americans] have spent all of their lives in this country, have attended the public schools where they have been instructed in the principles of democracy . . . and some of them are serving in the armed forces of the United States. To accuse them wholesale of disloyalty, as some people are now doing, is contrary to the letter and spirit of the American Constitution.

When some people began calling for the deportation of all Japanese Americans, Pratt responded,

> Of what crime are these people guilty? . . . the majority of them are guilty of no crime except that they or their ancestors were born in Japan. If this is a crime, then it is equally a crime . . . to have had German-born parents.

★ JAPANESE AMERICAN WRITERS ★
James Masao Mitsui

Mitsui's grandparents had emigrated from Japan to the Pacific Northwest. He and his family spent two years in the Tule Lake Relocation Camp in northern California, an experience that appears in several of his poems.

Mitsui taught high school English for thirty years. Along the way, he wrote three volumes of poetry, many of the poems dealing with family history.

Welcome Home?

When Japanese Americans returned to their homes, many found them in ruins. Landowners who had run prosperous farms and ranches found that their property had been vandalized. Business owners found that their assets had been sold off or run into the ground by "interim operators." Homes were vandalized, looted, or worse.

Wilson Makabe, an American soldier wounded in battle in Italy, came home to stunning news:
The family home had been burned down hours after the announcement that the internees would be returning. "All that time in the hospital I don't remember shedding a tear," said Makabe, "but I cried that night. . . ."

Not all the returnees faced hostility. In some communities, relief organizations worked overtime to find shelter for their former neighbors, and often families took returnees into their homes. Hundreds of returnees camped once again—this time in auditoriums, church halls, and public buildings —while they searched for a place to start their lives over.

Connections

- **Executive Order 9066**
- **Apology, Payment 48 Years in Making**
- **Photograph of a Child**
- **Destination: Tule Lake Relocation Center**

FOR YOUR READER'S LOG

In your Reader's Log, list the titles of the Connections that you are reading. After each one, write two things: (1) how the writer or speaker seems to feel about what is going on (even if the "feeling" seems to be a lack of emotion); and (2) your opinion of what was described.

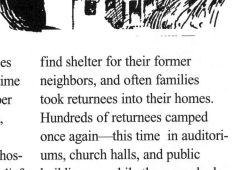
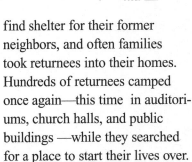

Name _____

Reading Skills and Strategies Worksheet

Book Organizer   *Farewell to Manzanar*

CHARACTER

Use the chart below to keep track of the characters in this book. Each time you come across a new character, write the character's name and the number of the page on which the character first appears. Then, jot down a brief description. Add information about the characters as you read. Put a star next to the name of each main character.

NAME OF CHARACTER	PAGE	DESCRIPTION

Reading Skills and Strategies Worksheet

Book Organizer *(continued)*   *Farewell to Manzanar*

SETTING

Where and when does this story take place? ....

....

....

CONFLICT (Read at least one chapter before you answer.)

What is the biggest problem faced by the main character(s)? ....

....

....

How do you predict it will be resolved? ....

....

....

MAJOR EVENTS

- ....
- ....
- ....
- ....
-

OUTCOME

How is the main problem resolved? (How accurate was your prediction?) ....

....

....

Reading Skills and Strategies Worksheet

Farewell to Manzanar

Foreword–Chapter 5: Listing Sensory Details

As the internees arrive at Manzanar and set up housekeeping, they experience many new sights, sounds, smells, tastes, and textures.

List as many sensory details as you can from this first part of *Farewell to Manzanar*. As you review the details, think about why living at Manzanar will be a challenge for the internees.

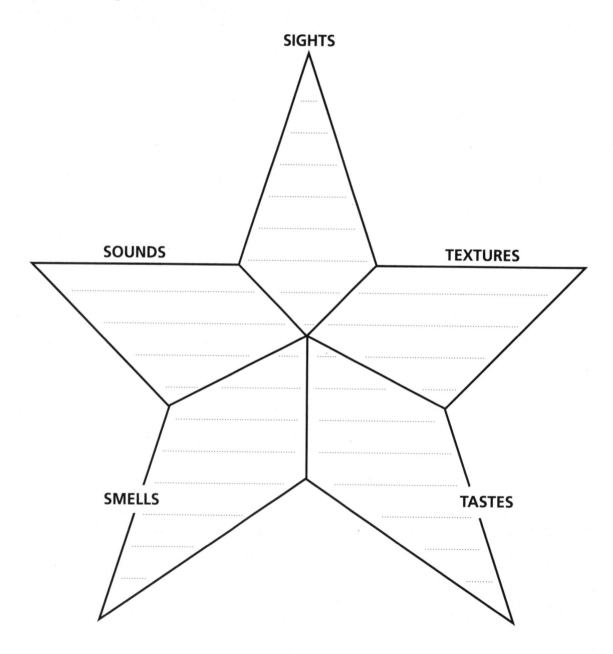

Reading Skills and Strategies Worksheet

Farewell to Manzanar

Chapters 6–11: Comparing and Contrasting Characters

Issei are first-generation Americans, born in Japan but living in the United States.
Nisei are second-generation Americans, born in the United States to Issei parents.
Think about the ways in which the Wakatsuki children (Nisei) are like and unlike
Papa and Mama (Issei).

In the separate parts of the ovals, write details that show how the generations differ in their personalities, values, and goals. Where the ovals overlap, note some ways in which the Issei and Nisei are alike.

BOTH

**PAPA AND MAMA
(Issei)**

**THE WAKATSUKI CHILDREN
(Nisei)**

Reading Skills and Strategies Worksheet

Farewell to Manzanar

Chapters 12–18: Identifying Problems and Solutions

When Chapter 11 ends, Manzanar is still quite a dismal place. From Chapter 12 on, however, some things begin to improve.

On the right, write how each of the problems is solved.

PROBLEM	SOLUTION
1. The family's living quarters are in a bleak, unattractive place.	
2. Papa needs something to do but won't take a job in camp.	
3. A farm is needed, but the water is drained off to supply Los Angeles	
4. Papa and Woody disagree about Woody's volunteering for military duty.	
5. The young internees need an education.	
6. Jeanne wants some special thing to do.	
7. The courts had not ruled on whether the detention was constitutional.	

Reading Skills and Strategies Worksheet

Farewell to Manzanar

Chapters 19–22: Responding to Quotations

What sentences in this section made you think of something in a new way? amused you? surprised you?

In the left-hand column, write interesting quotations from the text. In the right-hand column, write questions or ideas you have about the quotations.

QUOTATION	RESPONSE

Name _____ Date _____

Literary Elements Worksheet

Setting

The **setting** of a story—whether the story is made up or real—is the time and place in which the action occurs. In *Farewell to Manzanar,* the setting has a tremendous effect on the story.

Describe how each of the following elements of the setting affects Jeanne, her family, or the story itself.

ELEMENT OF SETTING	EFFECT
TIME: the attack on Pearl Harbor and the U.S. entry into World War II	
PLACE: the Japanese community on Terminal Island	
PLACE: Block 16 in Manzanar	
PLACE: Block 28 in Manzanar	
PLACE: the land around Manzanar	
PLACE: the apartment in Cabrillo Homes	
TIME/PLACE: Manzanar, 1972	

Name _____ Date _____

Literary Elements Worksheet
Farewell to Manzanar

Conflict

External conflicts are struggles with outside forces. **Internal conflicts** take place within the character's mind.

Describe three of Jeanne's external conflicts and two of her internal conflicts. Explain how each conflict is resolved. (If you feel that a conflict is not resolved, explain how Jeanne deals with it.)

EXTERNAL CONFLICT	RESOLUTION
1.	
2.	
3.	

INTERNAL CONFLICT	RESOLUTION
1.	
2.	

Literary Elements Worksheet

Flashback

Flashbacks are like taking trips back in time; they occur outside a story's chronological order. They can provide valuable background information and help the reader understand more about the characters involved.

Review the following flashbacks from *Farewell to Manzanar*. Then, write the information or insight you gained from each one.

FLASHBACK	WHAT I LEARNED
CHAPTER 6: Papa and Mama's background and marriage	
CHAPTER 6: Papa and Mama's silver anniversary	
CHAPTER 7: Papa's interview at Ft. Lincoln	
CHAPTER 22: Papa buys a car.	

Glossary

- Words are listed by chapter in order of appearance.
- The definition and part of speech are based on the way the word is used in the chapter. For other uses of the word, check a dictionary.
- **Vocabulary Words** preceded by an asterisk (*) appear in the Vocabulary Worksheet.

Chapter 1

*futile *adj.:* useless

*arrogance *n.:* pride combined with disrespect for others

*fruitless *adj.:* unsuccessful

*inkling *n.:* slight suggestion or hint

Chapter 2

translucent *adj.:* permitting light to pass through

*grueling *adj.:* very difficult or tiring

Chapter 3

*permeate *v.:* spread entirely through something

*subordinate *v.:* treat as less important

Chapter 5

tangible *adj.:* able to be sensed by touch

*gaunt *adj.:* very thin and bony

*awe *n.:* great wonder mixed with fear and respect

patriarch *n.:* male head of a family

Chapter 6

metamorphosis *n.:* complete change in form or structure

*derision *n.:* ridicule or scorn

entrepreneurs *n.:* people who open and organize their own businesses

*stalking *v.:* walking stiffly or arrogantly

*absurdly *adv.:* in a ridiculous or silly way

defer *v.:* give in to the opinion or action of another

*vanity *n.:* excessive pride in one's looks, abilities, or possessions.

*boisterous *adj.:* noisy and lively

*cronies *n.:* close or old friends

imperiously *adv.:* in a domineering or commanding way

Chapter 8

*concoct *v.:* cook; prepare

*pacify *v.:* calm or soothe

*leper *n.:* someone avoided for moral or social reasons

*cow *v.:* dominate by threats or shows of strength

cowered *v.:* crouched in fear

*tirade *n.:* long speech full of harsh, abusive language

contorted *adj.:* twisted into an unnatural form

*oblivion *n.:* state of forgetfulness or unawareness

Chapter 9

festered *v.:* caused bitterness over a long period of time

wholesale *adj.:* on a large scale; complete

*disperse *v.:* break up; scatter

Chapter 10

saboteurs *n.:* people, such as enemy agents, who try to hinder a nation's war effort

Chapter 11

*grotesque *adj.:* unnatural; bizarre

espionage *adj.:* spying

repatriation *n.:* returning people to their country of origin

*livid *adj.:* purplish color often caused by the stress of uncontrolled anger.

*plaintive *adj.:* expressing suffering or sadness

Chapter 12

*shrewd *adj.:* clever

*turmoil *n.:* state of great agitation or commotion

succulents *n.:* plants with thick leaves for storing water

*inevitable *adj.:* certain

alluvial *adj.:* having to do with soil deposited in a place by running water

Chapter 13

commemorated *v.:* remembered; honored

rapt *adj.:* completely absorbed

*exasperation *n.:* great annoyance or irritation

Chapter 14

*anxiety *n.:* worry over what might happen

hemorrhaged *v.:* bled heavily

detachment *n.:* feeling of separation

Chapter Fifteen

*dwindle *v.:* become steadily smaller

posthumous *adj.:* after death

Chapter 16

*rescinded *v.:* canceled

propaganda *n.:* ideas spread deliberately to further a cause

ominous *adj.:* threatening

*cringe *v.:* draw away in fear

*lethargy *n.:* indifference

Chapter 17

confiscated *v.:* taken away by authority

unnerving *adj.:* causing nervousness

*sustenance *n.:* means of support or nourishment

Chapter 18

tranquillity *n.:* peacefulness

inextinguishable *adj.:* unstoppable; unquenchable

Chapter 19

*volition *n.:* exercise of one's will; choice; decision

*disdain *n.:* feeling of deep dislike; contempt

*amorphous *adj.:* without a definite shape

Chapter 20

*acquiescence *n.:* acceptance; the act of giving in

intuitively *adv.:* with a direct understanding

*acknowledged *v.:* took notice of; responded to

Chapter 21

*persists *v.:* remains; stays

mediate *v.:* help opposing sides to reach agreement

incomprehensible *adj.:* impossible to understand

*ultimatum *n.:* final demand

inquisitively *adv.:* in a questioning way

sedate *adj.:* calm; serious

Chapter 22

inaudible *adj.:* unable to be heard

*incongruous *adj.:* not appropriate to a time or place

archaeological *adj.:* involving the scientific study of past human life and activity

*devoid (of) *adj.:* lacking

stunted *adj.:* kept from growing normally

*tenacious *adj.:* not easily uprooted or moved

deterred *v.:* stopped; held back

Name _____ Date _____

Vocabulary Worksheet 1 Foreword–Chapter 11

Farewell to Manzanar

A. In each blank write the Vocabulary Word from the box that best fits the sentence.

absurdly	boisterous	derision	grueling	stalking
arrogance	cow	pacify	leper	subordinate
awe	cronies	futile	livid	tirade

1. After the _____ training exercise, the actors stopped to rest.

2. The new director was _____ with anger at their performance.

3. He came _____ into the group and began a _____ that lasted nearly an hour.

4. It was clear that he wanted to _____ these actors and force them to _____ their wills to his.

5. Partly because of his vanity and _____ , his efforts were _____ .

6. The actors did not feel _____ at his status.

7. No one attempted to _____ him; instead, they expressed _____ .

8. Later, they joined their _____ and broke into _____ laughter at his expense.

9. The director noticed that he was being treated like a _____ .

10. He began to realize how _____ he had behaved.

B. Synonyms are words that have the same or nearly the same meaning. In each blank, write the Vocabulary Word from the list below that is a synonym for the word listed.

concoct	gaunt	inkling	plaintive
	fruitless		permeate
disperse	grotesque	oblivion	vanity

11. scatter _____

12. unsuccessful _____

13. brew _____

14. forgetfulness _____

15. distorted _____

16. hint _____

17. conceit _____

18. scrawny _____

19. mournful _____

20. penetrate _____

Vocabulary Worksheet 2

Chapters 12–22

Farewell to Manzanar

A. An analogy is a statement showing similarities between two pairs of words. The first pair of words in an analogy has the same relationship as the words in the second pair.

Complete the following analogies, using one of the Vocabulary Words below in each blank.

amorphous	cringe	inevitable	sustenance
	dwindle		persists
anxiety	incongruous	lethargy	ultimatum

1. success : failure :: calmness : _____

2. inescapable : _____ :: self-importance : conceit

3. sun : warmth :: food : _____

4. _____ : apathy :: jealousy : envy

5. replenish : increase :: use : _____

6. spherical : ball :: _____ : blob

7. continues : _____ :: joy : happiness

8. painful : enjoyable :: _____ : appropriate

9. _____ : suggestion :: command : request

10. shout : mutter :: jump : _____

B. Choose from the following list the Vocabulary Word that most closely matches each numbered word below. Write that word in the blank.

acknowledged	devoid (of)	rescinded	turmoil
	exasperation		tenacious
acquiescence	disdain	shrewd	volition

11. lacking : _____

12. compliance : _____

13. clever : _____

14. persistent : _____

15. annoyance : _____

16. recognized : _____

17. scorn : _____

18. choice : _____

19. disturbance : _____

20. repealed : _____

Name _____ Date _____

TEST PART I: OBJECTIVE QUESTIONS

In the spaces provided, mark each true statement *T* and each false statement *F*.
(20 points)

_____ **1.** After Pearl Harbor, Papa is arrested and taken to Washington, D.C.

_____ **2.** Rather than accept a dealer's low price for her set of porcelain, Mama smashes it to bits.

_____ **3.** During the first days at Manzanar, Mama tells jokes to keep up her family's spirits.

_____ **4.** The narrator includes a section about Papa's early life.

_____ **5.** Mama becomes a camp dietitian.

_____ **6.** Papa's drinking and bad temper occur because he knows he is dying.

_____ **7.** On the night that Papa threatens to kill Mama, it is Kiyo who stops him.

_____ **8.** Jeanne tries ballet and *odori* dancing, but she prefers baton twirling.

_____ **9.** After Manzanar, Papa takes a job at a fish cannery.

_____ **10.** When Jeanne visits Manzanar as an adult, she doesn't recognize anything.

Complete each statement by writing the letter of the best answer in the space provided. *(10 points)*

11. After the December Riot, Papa spends his time _____.
   a. caring for his family
   b. working at a camp job
   c. hiking, carving, and making a rock garden
   d. planning for life after the closing of Manzanar

12. A long-term result of the mess hall system at Manzanar is that _____.
   a. many internees do not get enough to eat
   b. family life begins breaking down
   c. young people gain weight by eating meals at two or three mess halls
   d. none of the above

13. Once life at Manzanar settles down, the camp administrators allow young internees to _____.
   a. receive mail
   b. go to school
   c. go on camping trips
   d. do all of the above

14. On Jeanne's first day in sixth grade, a classmate is surprised that Jeanne _____.
   a. can read and speak English
   b. is a Japanese American
   c. knows so many other students
   d. has just moved to Long Beach

15. Even after she becomes carnival queen, Jeanne realizes that _____.
   a. her mother disapproves of her
   b. the other students are jealous of her
   c. the only thing that she is good at is studying
   d. her classmates don't completely accept her

Study Guide | **47**

TEST   PART II: SHORT-ANSWER QUESTIONS

Answer each question, using the lines provided. *(40 points)*

16. Why were people of Japanese origin sent to camps?

_____

_____

_____

17. Why do some people in the camp think Papa is an informer?

_____

_____

_____

18. Depending on their answers to the loyalty questions, what three "gates" were open to the internees?

_____

_____

_____

19. How do you know that Bill, Tomi, Frances, and Martha Wakatsuki all answered YES YES?

_____

_____

_____

20. What scene shows Jeanne how deeply her parents care about each other?

_____

_____

_____

TEST PART II: SHORT-ANSWER QUESTIONS *(continued)*

21. Why does Papa decide to stay in the camp as long as possible?

....

....

....

22. When the Wakatsukis must leave Manzanar, why does Papa go out and buy a used car?

....

....

....

23. How does Jeanne respond when she learns that she can't visit some classmates' homes and can't join the Girl Scouts?

....

....

....

24. What are two of the things Jeanne succeeds at during her years in school?

....

....

....

25. Why does Jeanne try to forget about the camp for so long?

....

....

....

TEST PART III: ESSAY QUESTIONS

Choose *two* of the following writing topics. For each topic that you choose, use your own paper and write two or three paragraphs about the topic. (*30 points*)

a. Besides Jeanne, which two **characters** in *Farewell to Manzanar* do you think are most important to (1) the story's **conflicts** and (2) the story's **theme**? Explain your answers.

b. Do you sympathize with Papa, or do you condemn him for the way he acts? Using examples both from his earlier life and from his camp experience, make a case to support your opinion.

c. The **setting**—the time and place in which *Farewell to Manzanar* takes place—has a great effect upon the internees. Choose three elements of the setting. Explain how each makes a **conflict** in the book worse than it might have been otherwise.

d. What roles does Mama play in the camp? What is her impact on her family there?

e. Explain some ways this book has helped you understand more about other people or about yourself.

Use this space to make notes.

Answer Key

Foreword–Chapter 5
Making Meanings

READING CHECK

a. Papa is arrested under suspicion of delivering oil to Japanese submarines and taken to a detention center in North Dakota. The family is forced from Terminal Island and into Manzanar under the government's relocation program.

b. Answers may include the following: They are cold. Sand blows into their barracks compartment. They get sick from their typhoid shots and spoiled food. They have no privacy in their barracks or in the latrines.

c. Woody assumes the role of head of the household. He supervises as his younger siblings cover the knotholes in the floor and walls. He makes jokes and keeps up the family's hopes that matters will improve.

d. The children and adults often are separated during meals. The result is that families begin "sliding apart."

e. He has grown much thinner; he walks with a cane and seems to have aged ten years.

1. Most students will sympathize with the families and express frustration over the government's actions.

2. When her father is taken away, Jeanne is too young and confused to understand what is happening. She is probably the only family member who doesn't cry. When he returns, she is overwhelmed by how much he has changed and by her happiness at seeing him again. This time she is the only one who cries.

3. The students that threaten Jeanne and Kiyo are not Caucasian students but fellow Japanese Americans.

4. The full dinner set is a cherished and valuable possession. Mama smashes it in outrage that the dealers are taking advantage of her situation by offering far less money than the set is worth. This act also expresses her rage and frustration at the whole displacement process.

5. Much of "Almost a Family" deals with the loosening of family ties, shown by the contrast between family meals before the camp and at the mess halls. Still, the "Almost" indicates that in some ways the family is still a unit.

6. Students might suggest additional ways to keep the barracks warm in winter and cool in summer, ways to preserve the traditional family structure, or ways to make the camp seem more like home.

7. Students may conclude that in most life situations, cooperation is essential for any group of people to remain together.

8. Students may see the connection between the breakup of the family and Jeanne's postwar paper on the grunion hunt.

Chapters 6–11: Making Meanings

READING CHECK

a. Papa comes from a family of samurai, a tradition of highly respected Japanese warriors; Mama comes from a family of stonecutters. They marry by eloping, with the help of Mama's oldest brother.

b. They have a great feast, to which many friends are invited. Papa reigns over the activities like an emperor.

c. *Inu* means "dog" but is used also to refer to an informer or someone who cooperates with the enemy.

d. Kiyo stops Papa by punching him in the face.

e. The government wants the adults to sign an oath of loyalty to the United States, which means renouncing all allegiance to Japan.

1. Students' answers will probably vary. *Not surprised:* Going to the meeting fits with Papa's image of himself as a decision-maker. *Surprised:* Papa's behavior in camp up to this point has been to isolate himself and drink.

2. Students may cite, among other indications, the values of the samurai class that Papa had absorbed, his disapproval of his father's running a teahouse, his disdain for the fieldhands waiting for work in Honolulu, his tearing up the five-dollar bill after he had asked for a loan.

3. Papa is using a metaphor to refer to the fighting between Japan and the United States. Because he has strong feelings and loyalty to both, he doesn't want one to "kill" the other; he just wants the war to be over.

4 The bells may be ringing in memory of those who have been wounded or killed in the rioting, or they may be ringing as a sign of continued protest.

5. Especially because it happens at the time of the riot, the episode shows the fear and distrust between the two sides.

6. The last scene shows the internal conflict Papa feels between love for the country of his ancestry and heritage and the feeling that his future should be in the U.S.

7. Answers will be personal and need not be shared. Encourage students to consider both sides of the question, as discussed by Woody and Papa.

8. Students may recognize that their own birthdays and graduations (or bar mitzvahs, baptisms, etc.) bring together people who are important to them, create a sense of progress or achievement, make them feel included in a larger group, provide an excuse for having a good time.

9. Students may recognize that the flashback is important because it explains a great deal about Papa's background and Mama's deference to him.

Chapters 12–18: Making Meanings

READING CHECK

Events will vary but may include the family's move to Block 28, the class outing to Bair's Creek, Jeanne's *odori* lessons, the birth of Eleanor's baby.

The order of the three bulleted items:

- Jeanne wants to be baptized.
- The closing is announced.
- Woody visits Hiroshima.

You might have students verify each other's sequence of events.

1. Answers will vary.

2. The growing trees may symbolize the beginning of improved conditions in Manzanar or the growing hopes of a better life outside the camp.

3. The draft takes away many heads of families or young men upon whom other family members have come to depend. It causes a further breakup of extended families.

4. They are eager to leave the confines of camp and to have things that had been denied them during the internment. At the same time, many of them have lost their homes and their possessions and have no jobs waiting for them. In addition, they know that much anti-Japanese feeling remains, and they fear the future.

5. Answers will vary.

6. Students may suggest that physically changing our environments gives us a feeling of control and a feeling that we are making a difference. They may recognize that our surroundings affect the way we feel and even the way we behave. In a situation of deprivation, ugliness, and uniformity, gardens and a park give people something to look at and visit for pleasure, for a change from ordinary conditions. In some cases, like Manzanar, gardens and parks can remind people of their roots.

7. Some students may suggest that Woody doesn't recognize that he's crying, that he discovers it only when he feels the tears with his hand. In addition, this is a good example of *showing* rather than *telling,* a technique that makes the reader feel involved.

Chapters 19–22: Making Meanings

READING CHECK

a. Papa realizes that he is right back where he was in 1904: living in a new place and starting over from scratch.

b. A classmate is stunned to see that Jeanne speaks and reads English well. Her Japanese features make the classmate assume that she doesn't know much English.

c. Radine is immediately absorbed into the high school scene. Jeanne, though, can't be part of the social scene in the same way because a number of the teachers and the students' parents—and often the students, as well—do not consider her one of them.

d. Papa nearly dies from his abuse of alcohol. When he recovers, he returns to farming and moves the family to the agricultural region around San Jose.

e. She is first to finish college and first to marry someone who isn't Japanese.

---

1. Answers will vary. Students might be most surprised about Jeanne's desire to see Manzanar again.

2. Students may suggest that the scene shows that Papa still has "flourish," along with other personality traits such as pride that haven't been expressed in camp.

3. Jeanne doesn't want to be seen as Japanese (and, thus, an outsider). She struggles, however, because she also feels the need not to be invisible, to prove to others that she is every bit as "normal" as they are.

4. Papa dislikes seeing Jeanne so interested in American styles and customs instead of Japanese traditions.

5. Jeanne can't help feeling ashamed of the way she was treated; she can't stop feeling that it was her fault somehow. Shoving the experience to the back of her mind and trying to forget about it keeps her from those feelings of shame and guilt.

6. Students may cite the following effects of the visit: an appreciation for the men who had created a little bit of beauty with the rock gardens; renewed memories of the experiences of life there; the realization that "everything that had happened to me since we left camp referred back to it, in one way or another"; the realization that a small part of her still feels and may always feel shame at having been detained.

7. Answers will be personal and need not be shared. Encourage students to make some notes about their response and to save the notes for a possible future writing assignment.

8. Answers will vary; you might suggest listing both pros and cons.

9. While some students may feel that the flashback to the car purchase is a jolt, others may see that it plays several roles: It contrasts the two good-byes to the camp. It leaves the reader with the impact of the difficulties of the camp experience rather than the distance of Jeanne's memories. It brings the focus back to Papa, whose story this is in many ways.

Exploring the Connections

The Invisible Thread: **Making Meanings**

READING CHECK

Comments will vary but may refer to having a name that doesn't sound American and is difficult to pronounce correctly; having "Japanese" hair and dark eyes; feeling different from her schoolmates; having to make special requests (like "Do you cut Japanese hair?") when "regular" Americans would never do this; and being embarrassed when her parents act in keeping with Japanese traditions.

1. Some students may prefer to keep their responses to this question private.

2. Students will probably agree that the high point is the crossing of the Mississippi River.

3. The "compliment" makes Uchida realize that the woman had seen only her outer self and that this outer self would always be different. She understands that people who look only at the outer self will often make wrong assumptions.

4. She means that she learned the Japanese language simply from hearing her parents speak it.

5. Mama calls many things by the sounds they make. The vacuum cleaner, for example, is the *buhn-buhn;* a pair of scissors with a bell tied to it, the *chirin-chirin.*

6. Among the many ways their experiences are similar are their desire to fit in with the white majority; a series of experiences that show them people will usually see them as different; surprising people by their command of English; embarrassment at their parents' Japanese social customs; being encouraged by their parents to learn Japanese traditions—and resisting.

7. Answers will be personal and need not be shared.

Executive Order 9066: **Making Meanings**

READING CHECK

a. President Franklin D. Roosevelt issues the order.

b. Between December 7, 1941, and February 19, 1942, seventy-four days have passed.

c. The responsibility falls to the Secretary of War or to the Military Commanders under the Secretary's authority.

1. Executive Order 9066 is meant to lessen the risk of espionage and sabotage. It authorizes the establishment of military areas from which the military can force residents to leave. It requires that any such residents must be given food, clothes, and shelter and that other government departments and agencies must assist with this effort. It also provides means by which the order can be enforced. Student reactions will vary but are likely to be negative.

2. A *military area* is any area important to the war effort, such as the California coast—the area closest to Japan. Such an area might be strategically important if weapons or high-security defenses were developed there.

3. Roosevelt authorizes the use of Federal troops to help clear the military areas. He tells the Secretary of War to handle the situation and "to take such other steps as he . . . may deem advisable. . . ."

4. Excluded people are to be given food, shelter, transportation, medical help, supplies, equipment, and whatever else is needed. He does not go into more detail because at that time he doesn't know exactly what else will be required.

5. Students may point out that the document achieved the desired effect but that the government later needed to improve matters and, even later, to apologize to the internees. Students probably will feel that no one should be treated in such a way again.

Apology, Payment 48 Years in Making
Making Meanings

> **READING CHECK**
> **a.** She receives a check for $20,000.
> **b.** She also receives a letter from President Bush.
> **c.** His farm was sold to a white farmer. After the war, Tanaka worked on land that he used to own.

1. Students may suggest that the gesture was better than silence but that $20,000 could not possibly repay the internees. In addition to losing their homes, land, and personal possessions, they also suffered all the indignities that came with being considered "enemy aliens."

2. Answers may refer to the two-day period that Japanese Americans were given to gather their possessions and leave; the selling of property at a loss; the sufferings of living in tarpaper-and-tin shacks; and the fact that when they were released from the camps, their homes and land had been taken away from them.

3. It is ironic that the elderly Japanese Americans had to wait 48 years for the government to admit that it had made a terrible mistake. It is ironic that most of those who received the checks will use the money for medical payments and funeral expenses.

4. Some reasons for the ignorance about the internment camps are that students are often not taught about recent history; that many people who were involved did not want to think or talk about it afterward.

5. Students may suggest that government leaders should not only apologize but also praise the internees publicly for their courage, their loyalty, and their patience under stress. Students also may feel that the passing of time does not lessen the injustice.

Photograph of a Child / Destination: Tule Lake Relocation Center
Making Meanings

> **READING CHECK**
> **a.** He is taking a boat to the mainland as the first leg of his journey to a detention camp.
> **b.** She has been able to take very little with her; she has had to leave many of her cherished possessions behind.

1. Answers will vary. Students may feel more sympathy for the woman, as the child, like young Jeanne, is too young to understand what is happening.

2. The photograph probably showed a child among many adults on the pier, his hands holding his father's hand and the plane model, his head looking down. The writer supplied the sounds, what the child is trying to see, and what the child imagines.

3. The father's hand and ring finger represent the family security the child has in the confusing situation and the loss of his home. The U.S. fighter plane represents his Americanism and the irony that it is the U.S. that is sending him to the camp.

4. The woman is "wiping sight back" by wiping the tears from her eyes. To do this, she lifts her glasses and uses a wrinkled handkerchief.

5. The woman is absent-mindedly playing with a baggage tag. She is absent-minded because she is thinking about the home she leaves behind as well as her destination. The definition of *worry* that suits the situation best would be "to adjust repeatedly in a nervous or determined way."

Answer Key (continued)

Farewell to Manzanar

Foreword–Chapter 5: Listing Sensory Details

Answers may vary. Possible answers include the following items.

Sights: sharp Sunday blue, blazing eyes, yellow swirl, gaping knotholes, dust puffs, tiny volcanoes, moonlit surf, ghastly white, starched black hair, polished maple limb

Sounds: puttering engines, tiny white gulls, splattering rain, door wished open, convulsive tears

Smells: latrines, soap

Tastes: canned Vienna sausage, canned string beans, overcooked rice, canned apricots, home-grown vegetables, fish, boiled rice, soy sauce, horseradish

Textures: rough wooden floors, velvet case, dusty, icy gusts of wind, barbed wire, white lace, sweaty and grimy, wilted shirt

Chapters 6–11: Comparing and Contrasting Characters

Answers may vary, but they should be supported by the text.

Papa and Mama: conscious of social standing and class system within Japanese culture; dignified; sometimes reserved; firm ties to Japanese culture; goals are more ideal oriented; dreams of success are based on self-respect

The Wakatsuki children: Manzanar is a beginning; somewhat detached from Japanese culture; more focus on the individual; strong desire to be accepted by those outside the culture; goals are more material oriented; dreams of success driven by need for social approval

Both: strong family ties; drive to succeed; independent spirits.

Chapters 12–18: Identifying Problems and Solutions

Answers will vary.

1. Manzanar becomes less dismal for the family after their move to Block 28. Their living space is doubled, and they're now near an old pear orchard instead of the bleak desert landscape. Internees create gardens and a small park.

2. Papa cares for the orchard trees, makes furniture, creates a rock garden, paints and sketches, and dabbles with various hobbies.

3. The aqueduct taking water to Los Angeles is tapped into, and because the soil is rich, the farm thrives.

4. Papa and Woody reach a compromise. Woody can serve in the military if he waits to be inducted rather than volunteering.

5. A trained staff is hired, barracks are turned into schools, and school furnishings and supplies are provided.

6. She takes baton-twirling lessons, tries *odori* and ballet, and resumes her catechism.

7. The Supreme Court ruled that loyal citizens could not be detained against their will.

Chapters 19–22: Responding to Quotations

Quotations and responses will vary.

Setting

Answers will vary, but they should be supported by the text.

The attack causes worry and panic. It sets the relocations in motion.

The family is unaccustomed to living in a segregated community. Jeanne isn't used to seeing Asian faces.

They are horribly uncomfortable, overcrowded, and dismayed at living conditions.

Their living space is doubled, and the grounds are less bleak due to a nearby orchard. Jeanne finds life at Manzanar easier to bear once they move there.

The desert is forbidding and frightening to Jeanne and the other internees. It makes the fence almost pointless. It adds to their sense of isolation, physically and emotionally. The mountains, however, are a source of strength to some of the internees.

They can be self-sufficient now that they have a kitchen. The indoor plumbing is a relief after the facilities at Manzanar. Though some might find the building dreary, it is a new beginning for the Wakatsukis, a new home for them.

It's deserted and silent except for the wind. Most of the camp is gone, but the spirit from the period of internment lingers. Jeanne makes peace with this part of her life. She knows she cannot forget it, but she comes to terms with the impact Manzanar had on her and her family.

Conflict

Answers will vary, but they should be supported by the text.

External Conflict

1. Jeanne is picked on by some of the Terminal Island kids. **Resolution:** She and her older brother work out strategies.

2. Jeanne is a candidate for carnival queen, but the teachers and trustees don't want her to win. **Resolution:** A classmate reveals that teachers were planning to stuff the ballot boxes. Jeanne is crowned queen.

3. Papa does not want Jeanne to go to the coronation. **Resolution:** Jeanne agrees to take *odori* lessons.

Internal Conflict

1. She wants to be invisible and to feel accepted. **Resolution:** She takes part in many activities. She gets very good at baton twirling and goes on to join the baton club at school and to enter contests.

2. Her insecurities surface when one of the court attendants comments on her dress. **Resolution:** She concentrates on those who chose her to be carnival queen and gets through the event by reminding herself not to let them down.

Flashback

Answers will vary.

Chapter 6: This flashback gives the reader insight into why Papa is so devastated and changed by the detention experiences.

Chapter 6: Papa's behavior as host, the large amounts of food, the group of good friends all show the contrast between the family's life before and after the camp.

Chapter 7: This interview shows how well Papa handles himself in a difficult situation and how he automatically takes charge.

Chapter 22: The car-buying incident shows Papa's spirit, that his pride is still very much alive.

Vocabulary Worksheets

Vocabulary Worksheet 1

If you wish to score this worksheet, assign the point values given in parentheses.

A. *(4 points each)*

1. grueling
2. livid
3. stalking, tirade
4. cow, subordinate
5. arrogance, futile
6. awe

B. *(4 points each)*

11. disperse
12. fruitless
13. concoct
14. oblivion
15. grotesque
16. inkling

7. pacify, derision

8. cronies, boisterous

9. leper

10. absurdly

17. vanity

18. gaunt

19. plaintive

20. permeate

Vocabulary Worksheet 2

If you wish to score this worksheet, assign the point values given in parentheses.

A. *(5 points each)*

1. anxiety

2. inevitable

3. sustenance

4. lethargy

5. dwindle

6. amorphous

7. persists

8. incongruous

9. ultimatum

10. cringe

B. *(5 points each)*

11. devoid (of)

12. acquiescence

13. shrewd

14. tenacious

15. exasperation

16. acknowledged

17. disdain

18. volition

19. turmoil

20. rescinded

Test

Part I: Objective Questions

1. F	6. F	11. c
2. T	7. T	12. b
3. F	8. T	13. d
4. T	9. F	14. a
5. T	10. F	15. d

Part II: Short-Answer Questions

16. After Pearl Harbor, many people were afraid that people of Japanese origin would remain loyal to Japan and aid Japan in any way they could. The official solution was to isolate them in camps like Manzanar.

17. They suspect he cooperated too much with the authorities at the place he was first taken. Some students may cite more details: People knew that Papa had been a translator and that he had been released early, so the rumor started that he had reported on his fellow prisoners.

18. The three "gates" led to the army, Japan, or relocation (release from the camp). Some students may mention that another camp, Tule Lake, was a possible destination for those who were to be sent to Japan.

19. We know that they voted YES and YES because they eventually leave the camp and are relocated.

20. Students may cite either of two scenes: When the parents hear that Jeanne's sister and her baby are all right and they cry together or when Papa treats Mama's back pain with massage and the burnt cork.

21. Papa feels that he is too old to start life over again somewhere else. Then, too, living in the camp has become a comfortable way of life for him. All of his needs are met, and he doesn't have to face the loss of his home, his work, and his possessions.

22. Ever true to his samurai background, Papa refuses to be like "ordinary" people and take the bus.

23. Jeanne just accepts being rejected. Instead of feeling angry, she feels that it is somehow her fault.

24. Students should cite two of the following: good grades, becoming news editor of the school paper, being a majorette, being elected carnival queen.

25. Jeanne feels ashamed and guilty about having been there. She feels that in some way she is responsible.

Part III: Essay Questions

Students should respond to two out of the five essay questions. Answers will vary but should include specific references to the text.

a. Most students will choose Papa, with whom everyone seems to conflict and who survives the internment but is greatly changed by it. Mama and Woody are possible other characters, although not the only possibilities. Both conflict with Papa and show survival through determination and cheerfulness, respectively.

b. Many students will condemn Papa for his drinking, his fits of temper, his abuse of Mama, his constant brooding, and his refusal to take a job that he considers beneath him. Those who sympathize with Papa may do so because he never finds a perfect job (and thus a life worthy of his heritage) and because he is the target of insults and undeserved treatment (when all that he has done to be labeled *inu* is to be an interpreter).

c. The camp's isolated location increases the internees' feelings of abandonment and separation, thus making it easier for them to turn on each other, as in the December Riot. The sandstorms affect the internees' health and satisfaction with camp life. This worsens all their internal conflicts, such as their efforts to remain healthy and get on with their lives. The numbing cold and blistering heat, as well as the sad state of the accommodations, intensify the internees' conflicts with the camp administration.

d. Mama supports the family with money from her jobs inside and outside the camp. She also acquires the family's more spacious quarters in Block 28. Mama seems to influence Jeanne's life in subtle ways. For example, Jeanne says that she turns to Mama for reassurance, and she notes that Mama is always on her side when she does something that Papa doesn't like.

e. Answers will vary but should relate specifically to aspects of the book.

Notes

Notes